Why Do Germans Say That?

Copyright © 2021 Max Skalla and Werner Skalla. All rights reserved.
Published by Skapago Publishing, Von-Müller-Str. 12, 934347 Furth im Wald,
Germany. Contact to the publisher: info@skapago.eu, +49 9975 206330

Edited by Pilla Leitner & Werner Skalla
1st edition published in June 2021

No part of this publication may be reproduced, stored in a retrieval system, or transmitted in any form or by any means, electronic, mechanical, photocopying, recording, scanning, or otherwise, except as permitted by law, without the prior written permission of the Publisher. Requests to the Publisher for permission can be addressed to info@skapago.eu.

Links published in this book are accessible at the time of publication. The publisher cannot guarantee accessibility in the future.

ISBN Softcover: 978-3-945174-19-7
ISBN Hardcover: 978-3-945174-20-3
ISBN eBook: 978-3-945174-21-0

Free bonus materials to this book:
https://www.skapago.eu/jensjakob/idioms-bonus/

Learn languages with Skapago
German: Jens und Jakob, ISBN 978-3-945174-06-7
Swedish: Alfred the Ghost, ISBN 978-3-945174-10-4
Norwegian: The Mystery of Nils, ISBN 978-3-945174-00-5
Chinese: Oh, Jerry!, ISBN 978-3-945174-16-6

Other languages at www.skapago.eu

Why do Germans say that?
German expressions in comic strips

Text & illustrations
Max . Skalla

9 Edibles:
10 Alles in Butter
12 Senf dazugeben
14 Tomaten auf den Augen haben
16 Für n'Appel und n'Ei bekommen
18 Treulose Tomate
20 Auf den Keks gehen
22 Das ist mir Wurst
24 Honig um den Bart schmieren

27 Nations:
28 Alter Schwede
30 Spanisch vorkommen
32 Böhmische Dörfer
34 Sich freuen wie ein Schneekönig

37 Animals:
38 Da wird ja der Hund in der Pfanne verrückt
40 Da sagen sich Fuchs und Hase "gute Nacht"
42 Einen Kater haben
44 Einen Vogel haben
46 Eulen nach Athen tragen
48 Da liegt also der Hase im Pfeffer
50 Mein Name ist Hase
52 Schwein haben
54 Kein Schwein
56 Da lachen ja die Hühner
58 Der Hahn im Korb sein
60 Die Katze im Sack kaufen
62 Alles für die Katz'
64 Bock haben

67 Places:
68 Den Hof machen
70 Nur Bahnhof verstehen
72 Auf zwei Hochzeiten tanzen
74 Zum Lachen in den Keller gehen
76 Luftschlösser bauen
78 In Teufels Küche kommen

81 Clothes and body:
82 Das sind zwei Paar Schuhe
84 Den Gürtel enger schnallen
86 Ein alter Hut sein
88 Kleider machen Leute
90 Um des Kaisers Bart streiten
92 Die Daumen drücken
94 Zwei linke Hände haben

97 Colors:
98 Dasselbe in Grün
100 Blau sein
102 Blau machen

105 Objects:
106 Auf dem Teppich bleiben
108 Den Teufel an die Wand malen
110 Das Gras wachsen hören
112 Eine Flasche sein
114 Die erste Geige spielen
116 Etwas ist null-acht-fünfzehn
118 Etwas durch die Blume sagen
120 Spießer

122 Skapago

INTRO

www.skapago.com
If you took the time to tilt and read then drop by my website.
– I don't bite!

info@skapago.eu
Send me a message if you have any questions, or just to simply say hello.

Hallo,

my name is Max, and I moved to Germany in the pursuit of love and freedom, ironically around the perfect timing of a global pandemic.

I jumped into an adventure in the hopes of learning German – which is equally as confusing as German bureaucracy. Luckily I am enjoying my time deciphering the language and diving into German culture – albeit in lockdown. I learned through trial and error – reading stories or understanding a passing remark by a native speaker – which always led to coming face to face with the dreaded monster that you will definitely eventually face: "idioms" – the moment when you understand each word, yet have no clue what the hidden meaning is behind the words nor what is the origin story.

Therefore, I decided to use my lovely skill of child-like drawings to illustrate the meaning using different characters in a comic-style strip, while exploring the hidden story behind the expressions that even native speakers might scratch their heads in wonder to why do Germans actually say that.

I hope this book will shed some light on some German idioms, and be an experience as fun as I had creating it.

Enjoy.

EDIBLES

1. Alles in Butter
2. Senf dazugeben
3. Tomaten auf den Augen haben
4. Für n'Appel und n'Ei bekommen
5. Treulose Tomate
6. Auf den Keks gehen
7. Das ist mir Wurst
8. Honig um den Bart schmieren

– Are you ok?
– Everything in butter.

Alles in Butter

What? Literally: Everything in butter.
Means: Everything is fine.

How? Used to say that everything is going well, or great. Can be used as a reply when someone simply asks "how are you?" – "Alles in Butter." We can also use it in the negative form, for example "Alles ist noch nicht in Butter", meaning that everything is not or still not fine.

Why? Dipping valuables in butter sounds weird, but it was an effective way to transport valuables and fragile goods, such as porcelain or glasses, in the Middle Ages. It was a method of withstanding the bumpy roads while items were being transported by a horse-drawn carriage.
Another version of the story of origin comes from a marketing gimmick, as an innkeeper in Berlin displayed a sign noting that the food is cooked in butter, which was more valuable than other cheap fat alternatives.

– I told you not to put vases on the table!
– Do you also have to add your mustard?

Senf dazugeben

What? Literally: To put in mustard.
Means: To give unnecessary advice, or make unhelpful comments without being asked.

How? We all have that one friend who shares his opinion a bit too much, even when it is not the best time nor was the comment asked for. Of course you feel annoyed and comment "Do you have to put your mustard in?"

Why? Mustard was an imported spice from the Romans, and the Germans found it a bit spicy and strong, and in some dishes it was considered a stupid addition to the meal, similar to a weird unwelcome comment by someone.

– Do you have tomatoes on your eyes?

Tomaten auf den Augen haben

What? Literally: To have tomatoes over the eyes.
Means: Can't you see?!

How? You are sitting with your friend and having a nice warm tomato soup. Your friend says "Oh today was such a snowy day." – "What really? I did not notice." – "Do you have tomatoes on your eyes, you can clearly see the snow through the window." This fits me as I am someone who tends to trip on myself since I have bent feet. Of course this saying does not only refer to physically not seeing something, but also figuratively, as in "Do you have tomatoes on your eyes, of course this book is the funniest, best book I ever bought" – an inserted self promotion.

Why? A saying from the 20th century, probably has to do with being tired with red and puffy eyes from lack of sleep, red eyes and tomatoes, which meant people could not see well. Another funny possibility comes from the traffic police stopping people who run the stoplight, and they ask "Do you have tomatoes on your eyes?" as in "Did you not see the red light?"

– They are definitely expensive!
– I got it for an apple and an egg.

What? Literally: To get something for an apple and an egg.
Means: That was very cheap – price-wise.

How? You are strolling along the streets of Berlin, walk into a fancy shop and find a lovely set of elegant hats. You look at the price and think "Oh wow, this is a good price. I'll get it for an apple and an egg." It does not mean that something is cheap as in bad quality, more like a bargain, or as the Germans say: "ein Schnäppchen" – a catch.

Why? Imagine being in a rural area on a farm all the way back in the 17th century. If you have noticed that the idiom only mentions one apple and one egg, then you can imagine that it is very cheap, compared to a bunch of apples and eggs. Unless you mean Apple the brand then that would be a bit more expensive.

+ Note: This idiom is more commonly used in Northern German "Low German" dialect. You probably have noticed that the German word for apple is actually *Apfel*, except in the North it is *Appel*.

– I'm invited to watch football in the evening ... or should I stay?
– No, go ahead, you faithless tomato.

Treulose Tomate

What? Literally: Unfaithful tomato.
Means: Unfaithful, oh you're leaving me alone.

How? Used as an ironic expression that someone is not being faithful, or is ditching a planned event to do something else. Someone who does not show up for his appointments, ignores the phone and does not answer. You planned a gathering with friends this weekend to eat *Bretzel* and drink some beer. Everybody showed up except your friend Sarah von Hufenbauer. You call her up and say "Where are you, you unfaithful tomato?" Time goes by and you did not chat with her for a while, so you decide to send her a letter "How are you? It has been a long time, you unfaithful tomato."

Why? The love between a German and an Italian. This might possibly have to do with the First World War, as a term describing Italians. A time when Italy stayed neutral during the war, until it turned its position against the Germans in 1915. This combination with the fact that tomato harvest was not reliable in cold regions compared to Italy gave rise to the expression "You faithless tomato."

+ Note: Tomatoes in Austria are called "Paradeiser", because for a long time tomatoes were poisonous in these regions, and were only planted as ornaments in the garden. It was even sometimes called love apple – like Adam's apple in heaven.

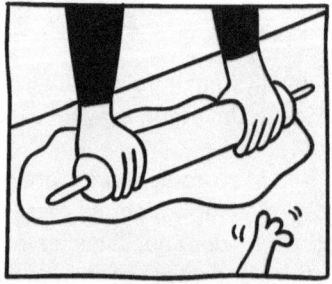

– You're going to me on the biscuit.

Auf den Keks gehen

What? Literally: Going on the biscuit.
Means: You are annoying.

How? When a person is getting on your nerves. Your boss is being overtly controlling, and today he wants you to do extra work "I am so annoyed. He is going to me on the biscuit." You are sitting at a lovely cafe with your best friend and he keeps complaining and you just want to enjoy your coffee and the famous Sachertorte "You are going to me on the biscuit, let's enjoy our time and complain later."

Why? Sadly one of my favourite idioms that happens to not have a concrete origin story. My theory as an avid home baker is that, of course I would be annoyed if someone walked on my cookies! I worked hard on them. Though Germans have different things that annoy them when you walk on them "Du gehst mir auf den Keks, den Geist – *spirit*, die Nüsse – *nuts*, die Eier – *eggs*…" Lesson is – If a German says you are walking on something, then probably they are annoyed.

– "A type of German sausage" or "pork sausage with curry ketchup"?
– Either or, it is sausage to me.

What? Literally: That is sausage to me.
Means: I don't care – whatever.

How? I heard this so many times, and was so confused when I heard it for the first time. I can't even remember the first time I heard it – since I probably have heard it now a thousand times. It basically means you don't care: "Would you like tea or coffee?" – "Either. It is sausage to me." It means something is also not interesting to decide, because it does not matter.

Why? Quite difficult to pinpoint the origin. It might have to do with butchers who did not know what to do with the leftover lower quality parts of an animal, so they decided to throw the parts into a sausage, because who cares – I actually do, but don't tell the butcher. It might also have a link with the saying "Everything has an end, only the sausage has two." Ironically Germans love sausages – therefore shouldn't the saying mean that something is very important? Like a sausage!

– Ticket please.
– Oh dear!
– You surely have beautiful eyes and a very beautiful voice.
– Do you want to put honey on my beard?

Honig um den Bart schmieren

What? Literally: Smear honey around the beard.
Means: To compliment someone – in order to benefit.

How? Your colleague Stein von Kussbart really likes to pamper the boss. He always gives compliments, gifts, and agrees on whatever the boss says. You gossip around coffee break with your other colleague and say "Herr von Kussbart smears the boss honey on the beard." Let's say you are trying to buy a new car, and the car dealer keeps pampering you while you are becoming annoyed "Don't smear honey on the beard, just answer my questions please." Though let's be honest here, we all smear a little bit of honey from time to time.

Why? It might actually have to do with the literal meaning of smearing honey on someone's beard, except it is not a person, rather a bear. It used to be a practice of bear tamers who gave bear dancing shows. They smeared honey around the mouth of the bear as a reward for a successful action. Though we can also find this behaviour in Chinese culture: smearing honey on the lips of a god figure in order to receive blessings.

+ Note: What if the person does not have a beard? Well, the German language is quite technical and efficient as we know. You can also say around the mouth "ums Maul, um den Mund" instead of a beard. Though *Maul* is a bit more rude than *Mund*, as it actually refers to an animal's mouth.

NATIONS

1. Alter Schwede!
2. Spanisch vorkommen
3. Böhmische Dörfer
4. Sich freuen wie ein Schneekönig

– Look!
– Old Swede!

Alter Schwede

What? Literally: Old Swede.
Means: Wow!

How? Used colloquially as a figurative speech for being surprised, or when something is shocking, for example: "Alter Schwede, did you hear the big news?" – "Alter Schwede, it was all over the newspapers."

Why? The term was used after the end of the Thirty Years' War, as Friedrich Wilhelm I of Brandenburg had Swedish soldiers recruited as instructors for the army. He was so impressed by how well they got along during drills that he started calling them "Old Swedes". The term is still commonly used after a couple of centuries. Apparently the Germans are not only impressed by IKEA, Abba, and Swedish meatballs, but also by Swedish soldiers.

– Why does he absolutely want to sell his car immediately?
– It seems Spanish to me.

Spanisch vorkommen

What? Literally: Seems Spanish.
Means: That is suspicious.

How? You open your email and find a message that reads "Hola, you have won the lottery, please send us your account number so we can transfer your money" – "Hm, that seems Spanish to me." Please proceed with caution, and if it happens to be a legit email I would kindly accept a 20% wire transfer as a friendly gesture.

Why? When the king of Spain Charles V, Holy Roman Emperor, ruled over Germany during the 16th century, many Spanish customs that were strange and bizarre to Germans came along as a natural consequence. Ironically reflecting a stereotype of the sceptical careful German, who needs to analyze what happens around him because even Spanish sounds suspicious.

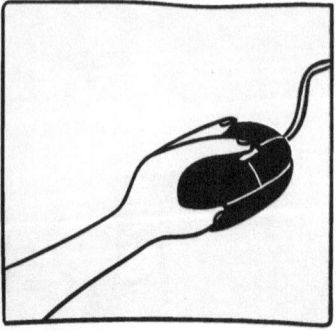

– Do you know HTML?
– These are Bohemian villages to me.

What? Literally: Bohemian villages.
Means: Something I don't understand at all.

How? When you have absolutely no knowledge of a certain field "like me sometimes during German class and I am sitting there puzzled with confusion." It is used to say that something is foreign to you, for example "Algebra is like Bohemian villages to me."

Why? This might be funny to hear if you happen to speak Czech. Germans who wandered around Bohemian villages during the Thirty Years' War could not understand the strange sounding village names, which became an expression of incomprehension and being lost. I find it quite amusing considering the incredibly long German words that sound incomprehensible to me. I guess I can make up my own new expression by saying "German villages."

– Was she happy about her present?
– Oh yes, like a snow king.

Sich freuen wie ein Schneekönig

What? Literally: To be happy as a snow king.
Means: To be really excited and joyful.

How? Every time we sit for lunch with the dog, he stares at us waiting for us to share a small piece of food with him. He stares until we finish eating, and then comes and starts pretending that he wants to get petted – when in fact he is only trying to see if there are any leftovers. Of course we saved up a small piece for him to eat, and you can see his eyes sparkling "He is as happy as a snow king." It describes this overwhelming joy one has, like the day of receiving birthday presents, or Christmas day.

Why? The expression actually has to do with winter, and a little cute bird named *Zaunkönig*, who has another common name *Schneekönig*. You can hear this bird singing despite the cold winter. The happiness that the bird expresses even through the harsh weather is the reason why this idiom is used.

+ Note: You can also say "as happy as a *Schnitzel*", "Ich freue mich wie ein Schnitzel", because *Schnitzels* make people happy.

ANIMALS

1. Da wird ja der Hund in der Pfanne verrückt
2. Da sagen sich Fuchs und Hase "gute Nacht"
3. Einen Kater haben
4. Einen Vogel haben
5. Eulen nach Athen tragen
6. Da liegt also der Hase im Pfeffer
7. Mein Name ist Hase
8. Schwein haben
9. Kein Schwein
10. Da lachen ja die Hühner
11. Der Hahn im Korb sein
12. Die Katze im Sack kaufen
13. Alles für die Katz'
14. Bock haben

– I can't work like that, the dog in the pan will go crazy.

Da wird ja der Hund in der Pfanne verrückt

What? Literally: The dog here will be crazy in the pan.
Means: This is crazy!

How? When something is so crazy that it is unbelievable and somehow unbearable. You are babysitting your neighbour's kids because you are a kind and helpful person. The kids start yelling, it escalates, and escalates ... and escalates, until you can't take it anymore "Oh this is crazy, for sure the dog will go crazy in the pan."

Why? A story of a dog named Hopf, whose brewer owner was invited to a wedding. He requested his friend Eulenspiegel to boil some hops while he was not there. Eulenspiegel was a very literal and accurate guy, so he threw the dog Hopf into the brewing pan instead of hops – do not worry, this was a joke story published in 1515. No dog was harmed during the writing.

+ Note: This expression is not used when something is crazy in a positive way. You can't say "The prices are so amazing, the dog is going crazy in the pan." It usually expresses either something negative, or something ironic.

– Where are we anyway?
– Here is where the fox and the rabbit say "goodnight."

Da sagen sich Fuchs und Hase "gute Nacht"

What? Literally: Here is where the fox and rabbit say "goodnight" to each other.
Means: This is in the middle of nowhere.

How? You are driving with your friend in a German village exploring a new unknown location. You look around and realize that you are both lost and in the middle of nowhere "Oh, here is where the fox and rabbit say goodnight to each other." And nope, do not be fooled like I was, and think it simply means "goodnight".

Why? A classic combination in fables and fairytales: the rabbit and the fox. There are many German sayings featuring either one of them. It's a combination that is rarely seen in real life, except in remote areas – therefore it turned into an expression that means a far and empty region.

- Yesterday.
- Don't you go to work today?
- I have a terrible tomcat.

Einen Kater haben

What? Literally: To have a tomcat.
Means: Having a hangover.

How? You drank too much beer at *Oktoberfest*, woke up the second day hammered and you think "Oh God, I feel horrible, I have a tomcat." Or you can have a sophisticated beer tasting in Bavaria, just don't overdrink, or else you will get a male cat, but ironically not a female cat.

Why? You visit your doctor know-it-all friend and you say, "Oh man, I am hungover." He looks at you and replies "Ah, you have Katarrh", which is a medical term that shares similar symptoms to a hangover with some headache, runny nose, a cough, and that awful feeling of being sick. The similar pronunciation to *Kater* developed into this expression, probably because they were too hungover to properly pronounce *Katarrh*, which to my ears sounds like *Qatar*.

– What is he doing?
– He has a bird.

Einen Vogel haben

What? Literally: To have a bird.
Means: This is crazy – that's cuckoo.

How? When someone is completely nuts. You walk in the street and you see a shop with a 99% discount and think "They have a bird that is cuckoo." You meet your friend at the park and he asks you, "Do you think Olga is cute?" and you reply, "Do you have a bird? She is married."

Why? An old superstition and expression that insane people have birds nested on their head, in a literal sense. Figuratively speaking the birds are chirping in your head and you can't think clearly. It was an actual word describing insane people, that expanded to include people who said something dumb or did something stupid. I have to say, as someone who loves birds, I guess I am always crazy.

– Flowers flowers.
– It's like carrying owls to Athens.

Eulen nach Athen tragen

What? Literally: To carry owls to Athens.
Means: To do something unnecessary, or unreasonable.

How? You are invited to a birthday party at your friend's house, who happens to be a chocolate store owner. You bring a bar of chocolate as a gift, and your friend opens his gift, smiles, and thinks to himself, "What an odd gift, I already have a whole shop of chocolate. It is like carrying owls to Athens." This can also describe a political action, or any unreasonable act that is unnecessary.

Why? From a comedy that dates back more than two thousand years by a Greek writer Aristophanes. The owl was not only a symbol of the Goddess of Athens, but also a symbol of wisdom presented in art, poetry, and even on coins – you can even still see the owl on a 1 euro Greek coin to this day. And due to the abundance of owls "money" in Athens, it was considered unreasonable to bring more owls to the city, something along the idea of "supply was high and demand was low." Of course, I would not have minded more owls "money" in my bank account, if you had asked me.

– Start the car.
– So there's the rabbit in the pepper.

Da liegt der Hase im Pfeffer

What? Literally: Here lies the rabbit in pepper.
Means: Aha, so this is the real reason.

How? Let's say you have a gut feeling that something is suspicious, for example: when your friend is acting a bit too nice, and then suddenly asks if he can borrow some money, and you think to yourself "Aha, so that is why he was being so nice." Of course I would still hear my friend out, maybe he needs the money, be nice. It can also express that you found a solution to a problem, "My computer is not working" – "Aha, the plug was not connected."

Why? A popular meal called *Hasenpfeffer* – rabbit pepper that dates all the way back to the 13th century. The taste of the pepper spice in the sauce was so strong that it overpowered the rabbit meat, and once people tasted the meat they replied with "Aha, so here lies the rabbit in the pepper." I usually avoid meat, so I guess in my case it would be "Aha, so here lies the tofu in the pepper."

+ Note: Check out the story of the idiom "Spanisch vorkommen" that led to the situation described in this one.

– Where are my carrots?
– My name is rabbit, I know nothing.

Mein Name ist Hase

What? Literally: My name is rabbit.
Means: I don't know – Pretending to be innocent.

How? You are watching an interview with a celebrity who is being asked about some rumours or scandals about him partying and drunk driving. He replies to the interviewer with "My name is Rabbit." It usually is a response to an accusation, or someone being suspected of something.

Why? An incident in the mid 19th century, of a student in Heidelberg named Karl Victor Hase, who helped a friend flee to France by assisting him with identity fraud. Unluckily for Mr. Hase he was caught by the authorities, and during his interrogations his response was "My name is Hase, I reject the questioning, I know of nothing." The lucky suspect was set free, and the statement became so popular that it was used in pop culture as a reference. I find it cute that an actual person existed with the name Mr. Rabbit.

+ Note: It is commonly used in this combination "my name is Rabbit, I know of nothing" – "Mein Name ist Hase, ich weiß von nichts."

– You surely had (a) pig.

What? Literally: To have (a) pig.
Means: To get lucky.

How? A general meaning to describe a situation where someone got lucky! You are walking on the street and a bicycle passes by, and you were a split second from getting hit – "You had a pig." Or you were one mark from failing your German test – "You have a pig."

Why? The pig was for a long time a symbol of being wealthy, or having a business. Pigs brought income to families and meant they were less poor than their neighbours. I mean, we all know the cliche of Germans and their love of *Wurst*. You can even see it in the Middle Ages in festivals with a consolation prize for the worst participant with a pig, an unexpected lucky surprise for the loser. As for me, I prefer to stay away from meat, so maybe I should say "I have tofu."

– No pig can read that.
– No pig wants to eat that.
– No pig is interested.

Kein Schwein

What? Literally: No pig.
Means: Nobody! Not a single person.

How? When you want to emphasise that really nobody at all can do something, or even has the interest. "You are crazy, no pig can say *Eichhörnchen* five times in a row." You are watching with your friend a documentary about the history of bubblegum, and your friend comments "Why are you watching this boring topic? No pig is interested" – I actually find that interesting, so maybe we can create a new expression: "One pig is interested."

Why? Interestingly, the origin of the saying has absolutely nothing to do with pigs, rather a man called Mr. Swien who lived in Schleswig-Holstein in Northern Germany. He possessed a magical skill called reading and writing. He earned his money by performing his magic during the late Middle Ages for the people in the area. And when Mr. Swien could not understand the text, the customer would say, "Not even Swien could read this."

+ Note: You might also hear "Keine Sau." It has the exact same meaning. You can only use this form in the negative. You can't say "a pig can read this," it has to be "no pig can read this."

– Dad says we all descended from apes.
– Such nonsense, the chickens are laughing.

> Da lachen ja die Hühner!

What? Literally: The chickens are laughing here for sure.
Means: That is ridiculous!

How? You are reading the newspaper and you see a title that says "Learn German in 3 months." You find that ridiculous. "The chickens are laughing here for sure." It describes something so absurd that even chickens would laugh. Of course I am not bashing learning a language in 3 months at all. We all have the right to build air castles – see page 76.

Why? There are some documented writings in the early 20th century with this idiom. If you happen to live on a farm with chickens, you might have noticed that the sounds they make are similar to human laughter – unless German chickens laugh with an *Umlaut*. You can even see the link with the German word describing the sounds of chickens cackling *gackern*, which is also used colloquially to say *laughing*.

– So what's it like ...
– ... as a rooster in the basket during aerobics class?

Der Hahn im Korb sein

What? Literally: To be the rooster in the basket.
Means: Being the only guy in a group of girls.

How? When a guy is the only male in a project full of girls, and his jealous wife comments with a hint of cynicism, "Uh-huh, so you are the rooster in the basket." It is a general description of being the only boy enjoying the full attention of a group of girls.

Why? Quite a literal description of how a rooster is the leader surrounded by a group of chickens. The basket is a reference to the barn, or yard where the chickens live. It could also have a connotation to a time when chickens were carried to the market in baskets.

– A new restaurant is open.
– Surprise menu, yummy cat.
– I don't really want to buy the cat in the sack.

Die Katze im Sack kaufen

What? Literally: To buy the cat in the sack.
Means: To buy something without verifying the quality of the product in advance.

How? You are browsing the internet on your mobile at 12 pm instead of sleeping like a responsible person, and you see an ad that says, "Buy our magic pillow and you will sleep better – no refunds accepted" and you think to yourself, "What a horrible ad. They want me to buy the cat in the sack." You can even sometimes see an ad that says, "Do not buy the cat in a sack, because we offer samples."

Why? We all know the feeling of buying a sack of meat from the store and being scammed by cat meat instead, or do we? That is supposedly the fear people had around at least 500 years ago, as fraudsters would swap meat and sell it to poor unsuspecting customers. Poor cat in a sack ...

– Oh dear! It's raining.
– That was all for the cat.

Alles für die Katz'

What? Literally: Everything for the cat.
Means: That was all in vain – a waste of time.

How? Oh, the reality of life. We work hard. We spend energy and time, then we realise that "Everything was for the cat." It expresses this feeling of frustration we have when we tried our best yet failed, or it didn't go as planned. When you spend your day cooking for a party, then your friends cancel at the last minute. "My whole day was spent in vain. It was all for the cat."

Why? This might have to do with leftover food that is given to street cats. A story in the 17th century from Abraham a Santa Clara, who receives promises from his master instead of being paid. The poor man had a cat he could not feed. The cat eventually starved to death, and the man commented, "My cat died from promises". Another very generous and kind-hearted blacksmith in a fable from 1548 by Burkhard Waldis in "Esopus", who was naive to let his customers decide how much they wanted to pay for his services. Some ungrateful customers thought a mere thank you would suffice, and yet again the blacksmith had worked hard for nothing, and could not feed his cat. Poor cats – that was all in vain.

– Should we go to the cinema?
– No, I don't have a male goat for cinema.

Bock haben

What? Literally: To have a male goat.
Means: Would like to do something.
The opposite would be "keinen Bock haben."

How? "I have such a male goat on reading *Lustiges Taschenbuch** today" – I actually recommend them for learning German if you already have a good level. The idiom expresses the desire to do something, or expresses the lack of desire also: "I have no male goat for watching a movie tonight, let's eat out instead." You might also run into this expression on marketing campaigns: "No male goat on attending a German course? Then try out Skapago and learn online instead" – an actual website I recommend for language learning online.

Why? A dialectal expression from the 70s from the word *Bokh* in Romani, which means *hunger*. The term gradually infiltrated the young hip culture of the time, and the similarity to the word *Bock* got popular and is still used to this day.

+ Tip: You can also say "Null Bock", as in zero desire to do something.

* Donald Duck comics.

PLACES

1. Den Hof machen
2. Nur Bahnhof verstehen
3. Auf zwei Hochzeiten tanzen
4. Zum Lachen in den Keller gehen
5. Luftschlösser bauen
6. In Teufels Küche kommen

– Do you think he wants something from you?
– Of course, he's been making the royal court for me for weeks.

Den Hof machen

What? Literally: To make the royal court.
Means: Giving signals that you want to date – to court someone.

How? You want to flirt, and express your emotions to that lucky someone, so you open the door for them, buy flowers, and send them surprise chocolate gifts. You are "making the royal court for them". It can also be used in a cynical manner as in "A political party is making the royal court for someone" – as in they are courting and trying to please.

Why? A possible French loanword from "faire la cour à quelqu'un" which means, serving the royalty. The court "Hof" were the aristocrats surrounding the king. This became a description of a man who is "courting" a woman and pleasing her like they did to the royalty. This meaning expanded to cover both romantic and political pleasing.

– A train station.
– What … ?!
– … I only understand train station.

What? Literally: Only understand railway station.
Means: I do not understand a thing.

How? You just finished your A1 level class and you are waiting at the lovely *U-Bahn* station. You start hearing an announcement in German and you can barely understand due to the noise and lack of extensive German vocabulary, therefore you think to yourself, "I have no clue what he just said. I only understand railway station."

Why? During the First World War, the soldiers were completely exhausted and were fed up by the fighting and the war, and were dreaming of a train ride back home. They did not want to talk, nor were they interested in small talk. Each time they were asked something about the war, or any other topic, they simply replied "I don't know, I only understand railway station." This saying survived to this day as an expression of not understanding. My stepfather actually loves trains and has a model railway train at home, and each time he talks about it I zone out and think to myself "I don't even understand railway stations."

- I am ready for my ballet class.
- But we are invited to the birthday party.
- You can't dance at two weddings.

Auf zwei Hochzeiten tanzen

What? Literally: To dance at two weddings.
Means: Doing two incompatible things at the same time.

How? Your boss wants you to finish the project by tomorrow, but you also have to attend a seminar for work that lasts a couple of hours. You look at your boss and say "This is impossible. I can't dance at two weddings." It is a reference that two things cannot happen at the same time. Though you can be creative and try to solve the problem "I want to dance at two weddings. I will watch the live concert on TV, and do my homework at the same time."

Why? An old German saying: One cannot marry more than one person at the same time, therefore one cannot celebrate two things at the same time. The wedding is the highlight and the celebration of the love between a couple, one must give his attention to it, and not be distracted by something else.

– Why does he never laugh?
– For sure he goes to the cellar to laugh.

Zum Lachen in den Keller gehen

What? Literally: To go to the basement to laugh.
Means: Someone who doesn't have humor – never laughs in public.

How? You are sitting with a friend at your German course, and you tell him a joke "Zwei Martini bitte." – "Dry?" – "Nein, zwei!" He looks at you and doesn't laugh because he is too serious and wants to focus on the course and not waste his time on your jokes, but don't worry, "He goes to the basement to laugh." He could be too embarrassed to laugh in public, or maybe he should attend more German courses to understand the joke.

Why? Probably dates all the way back to the 1920s. The idea that a humorless person only goes to the basement to laugh, in order to make sure that nobody hears him. After all, a serious person does not like to be seen as silly and fun. I would rather take my friends and laugh together in the basement, break the cliche.

– Are you still building castles in the air,
  or are you making nails with heads?

Luftschlösser bauen

What? Literally: To build castles in the air.
Means: Having unrealistic dreams – without executing them.

How? This moment when you are lying on the grass, dreaming that one day, far in the future, you will be able to pronounce long German words without having to take a pause every two syllables: "You are building castles in the air." Of course this idiom does not fit if you have bought this book, because to the contrary it shows that you are actually making an effort to learn. This is one of my favorite idioms. I find it a bit magical, and we all need a sense of imagination, even if it might be unrealistic.

Why? A popular idiom from the 17th century, a classical stereotype of a German who likes to plan every single detail. A castle needs a foundation, planning, management, and hard work, and as you can imagine air is not a solid foundation to build on. My counter argument would be that even if you want to build a castle, you still need to have some fantasy. After all, we do need to dream in order to plan.

+ Note: "Nägel mit Köpfen machen" – *to make nails with heads* is another idiom that means "to execute a solid plan." It is the exact opposite of "Luftschlösser bauen."

– The boss is here. Should I tell him the bad news?
– Don't do that, you'll come into the devil's kitchen!

In Teufels Küche kommen

What? Literally: To come into the devil's kitchen.
Means: To get into a very troublesome situation.

How? Your best friend is a naive person, who believes that everybody has a good heart. He decides to tell his friend Emma von Hufenbauer from kindergarten that he stole her favorite yellow crayon, but then you remind your best friend that Emma is a bit crazy and might react very badly, and he definitely "will come into the devil's kitchen."

Why? If you happen to have read the Brothers Grimm – if you did not, I fully recommend them in German: creepy but fun – then you might notice the connotation of Devil and kitchen: The witch who brews potions in her big cauldron from the story of Hänsel und Gretel, who the witch lured with candy in order to cook them. I mean, the devil is hot, and I guess you need some heat in order to cook.

CLOTHES & BODY

1. Das sind zwei Paar Schuhe
2. Den Gürtel enger schnallen
3. Ein alter Hut sein
4. Kleider machen Leute
5. Um des Kaisers Bart streiten
6. Die Daumen drücken
7. Zwei linke Hände haben

– Do you want to go to the concert tonight?
– The tickets are expensive.
– Whether you want to or whether the tickets are expensive are two pairs of shoes.

> Zwei paar Schuhe sein

What? Literally: These are two pairs of shoes.
Means: These are two different things.

How? When two things are so different, they are not even comparable. You are reading an article online that says having money means being happy, and you think to yourself "These are two pairs of shoes, just because you have money doesn't mean you are happy." Or someone mentions that you have to be tall in order to be successful "Height and success have nothing to do with one another, they are two pairs of shoes." Though I wouldn't mind being tall, being happy, and having money, at least I would buy me some fancy pairs of shoes.

Why? Might happen when you wake up sleepy, and wear two different shoes by accident – one brown and the other one black. If you ask me I would say "That sounds fabulous, wear them with pride."

+ Note: You can also say "Das sind zwei Paar Stiefel" – *boots* instead of shoes.

– Now we have to tighten our belts.

Den Gürtel enger schnallen

What? Literally: To tighten the belt.
Means: Tough times are coming, we need to reduce expenses.

How? You are living a busy student life and have no time for a side job and your bank account looks like mine, and you think to yourself "I don't have a lot of money this month, I'm gonna have to tighten the belt."

Why? A writing in the 19th century references this idiom, that hard times are coming and people have to tighten the belts. It has a literal meaning that you can imagine, when someone is starving and loses weight, and therefore has to tighten his belt because his pants are slipping off. There is also a common myth that tightening belts reduces the feelings of hunger. Quite a sad idiom, but we might all have faced a moment or two of struggles and had to tighten our expenses too. I like to wear elastic waisted pants, so no need for belts.

– I heard bell bottoms are all in now.
– Oh, that's an old hat, we had that back in the 70s.

Ein alter Hut sein

What? Literally: To be an old hat.
Means: Mainstream, everybody already knows, not trendy.

How? You are sitting with your friend and he tells you a joke, you reply "That is an old hat, I heard this when I was in kindergarten." You can sometimes see an article that says something like "Is this a new trend or an old hat?" Even though I like vintage hats and find them cute.

Why? It is quite interesting how trends come and go. Especially when I see old photos in black and white with people wearing hats, which nowadays would be considered old fashioned and out of place. Interestingly enough, the idea of hats going out of style is not a modern phenomena. Johann Gottfried Pahlin wrote in 1799 about someone who he criticized as being too old fashioned to be discussing trendy topics in society by saying "He was so out of style, like an old hat." – such a witty insult.

– Clothes make the people. Number 3 fits a job interview.

Kleider machen Leute

What? Literally: Clothes make people.
Means: Wearing suitable clothes to impress, or pretend.

How? You are what you wear. If you want to impress someone or pretend to be someone you are not, then clothes are a good start. You open a magazine and it says "Clothes make people: are black shirts the best choice for a job interview?" You ask your muscular friend to share with you advice about losing weight and he says "Clothes make people. Wear sports clothes." – of course that doesn't work, but at least it will put you in the mood to work out.

Why? A very old idiom that is shared in many languages over the centuries with slight variations. The Swiss poet Gottfried Keller wrote a story in the 19th century titled *Clothes make the man*. The story describes a poor tailor who was mistaken for a Polish count because of his elegant clothes, though he eventually gets exposed. Ironically, we all try not to judge people by their appearance, yet we are always recommended to dress to impress.

- She is planting carrots.
- No, tomatoes.
- They are arguing about the emperor's beard.

Um des Kaisers Bart streiten

What? Literally: To argue about the emperor's beard.
Means: To argue about something irrelevant – because it is not your business.

How? I have always wondered why people like to argue over other people's business. You are hanging out with a group of friends and they are all arguing on whether Brad and Angelina should or should not break up, one gets angry, the other one starts to shout, another is crying on the corner yelling "Why ... WHY", and you are sitting in the middle thinking "They are fighting over the emperor's beard." It also describes a dispute over a trivial and insignificant matter.

Why? Researchers are still arguing over the emperor's beard about the origin of the emperor's beard. For many centuries artists depicted emperors with a beard or without, as they were not sure whether they were shaved or not and which color the beard was. This caused the public to argue about the legitimacy of the depiction of how the emperor looked – because we all know how important a beard is. This happened to Emperor Charlemagne, and Emperor Friedrich I Barbarossa. If you ask me, maybe Caesar shaved his beard sometimes, therefore both arguments are accurate.

– Czech little box of matches.
– Good luck with the language test - I'll push the thumbs to you!

Die Daumen drücken

What? Literally: To push the thumbs.
Means: To wish someone luck – crossing fingers for someone.

How? A classic response to show support to someone for doing a task. My healthy, super-muscular friend is running a marathon and my response is as usual "Oh man, this sounds tough. I push the thumbs to you." Or in my case when I needed to pass my German driving exam and my supportive friends would say "Good luck. I push my thumbs to you."

Why? A gesture of mercy in ancient Rome. When a gladiator lost a combat, he would raise his index finger pleading for mercy from the audience. If the audience chose death, then they would raise their thumb. If they chose to pardon, they would clinch their fists with their thumb down. There is also an old Germanic superstition and belief that the thumb possesses magical powers. Therefore, they would hold the thumb down in order to prevent it from negatively influencing the other person.

– You surely have two left hands.

Zwei linke Hände haben

What? Literally: To have two left hands.
Means: Being clumsy.

How? Describes an awkward person who is not good with tools or does something clumsy. You bought a table from Sweden, and now you need to put the pieces of the table together "Oh I understand the IKEA instructions, but I have two left hands", which means you are clumsy and incapable of using the tools.

Why? A popular creative expression from the 19th century, which is probably borrowed from France – the classic feud between the English and the French. It is mentioned in a German publication from a politician named Honoré Gabriel de Riqueti, comte de Mirabeau about the clumsy English by saying "They have two left arms." The poet Heinrich Heine commented about the still clumsy English who travel to France in order to learn to speak and move, and in their return they no longer have two left hands, nor are satisfied with beef steak and plum pudding.

+ Note: In a play of words "I have two right hands" means the complete opposite, that someone is quite skillful and talented. It was a description used for talented pianists. A review of a concert by Sigismund Thalberg says: "Thalberg has no left hand, he has two right hands, and more."

1 Dasselbe in Grün
2 Blau sein
3 Blau machen

– What is the difference?
– It's the same in green.

> Dasselbe in grün

What? Literally: The same in green.
Means: The same, or something very similar.

How? Basically an idiom that means something is similar, or almost the same. You check an ad for a mobile brand with the number S94. You wonder what is the difference with the last release S93 and you realise "They are very similar, the same in green." Of course the actual difference is the double digits on the price tag.

Why? It might have come from the automotive industry from 1921. The French brand Citroën released CV5 model, and a couple of years later the German car brand Opel released 4 PS called "Tree frog". The car looked like an exact copy except in green. Hence "The same in green." A very cute car – you should look it up.

– She is blue.

Blau sein

What? Literally: To be blue.
Means: To be drunk.

How? It is New Years, and your friend drank too much and started slurring and dancing funny. Your comment would be "Oh he is so blue." You can connect another idiom together: "My friend is so blue, tomorrow he is definitely going to have a tomcat."

Why? You would like to dye your beautiful white shirt in the Middle Ages to blue. You would need some sunshine, a plant called *Färberwaid*, and a group of men to urinate in a bucket. Apparently urine was needed in order to create the blue color dye when it reacted with the plant, and in order to create as much urine as possible, they opted into drinking and … to tinkle in the bucket. I guess I would have avoided the color blue in the Middle Ages.

– School!
– I am sick …
– Oh what, you sure are just making blue.

Blau machen

What? Literally: Making blue.
Means: To skip school, or work.

How? You are at work and checking out Facebook messages – like every good hardworking person would do, and you see your friend's post who skipped work and is enjoying his day at the park "Oh, he is making blue."
Your lucky friend did not show up to school today "Oh wow, he is making blue!" The idiom is used to express that someone has avoided their responsibility by enjoying their time and skipping work or school.

Why? This has to do with the same origin story mentioned in this book about the expression "being blue". First the workers soaked the fabric on a Saturday, then would wait until Monday to hang the fabric in the air for it to dry. And as they waited for the fabric to fully turn blue, they had nothing else to do other than hang out and relax. Hence "making blue".

+ Note: *Blaumachen* is actually a separable verb "Ich habe heute blaugemacht" – "Willst du blaumachen?" – "Sie macht heute blau."

1 Auf dem Teppich bleiben
2 Den Teufel an die Wand malen
3 Das Gras wachsen hören
4 Eine Flasche sein
5 Die erste Geige spielen
6 Etwas ist null-acht-fünfzehn
7 Etwas durch die Blume sagen
8 Spießer

– I am moving out!
– Now stay on the carpet ...
– ... I just said that I can't sleep with your snoring.

Auf dem Teppich bleiben

What? Literally: To remain on the carpet.
Means: Be reasonable, you are exaggerating.

How? When you get great news that you won the lottery and you start screaming and jumping around and your friend says "Remain on the carpet" – remain down to earth, do not rush and let's get all the details first. Or it can also be in a negative situation, when for example you receive horrible news that you lost the lottery and you start crying and banging on the walls and your friend says "Remain on the carpet" – do not explode and keep your composure.

Why? It probably has a connotation to the context of carpets being classy and posh, which lead to the use of this word to mean "Calm down, handle this in sophistication" like a beautiful Persian rug would do.

– Who knows, maybe the police are waiting for us outside?
– Now stop, don't draw the devil on the wall!

Den Teufel an die Wand malen

What? Literally: To draw the devil on the wall.
Means: To talk about something bad that might happen – which manifests it to reality.

How? My German friend is an adventurous and spontaneous person. We decided to skydive, so the first thing he does is to go online and search the statistics of skydiving injuries. He calls me up and starts mentioning all the horrible things that might happen, the classical "what if …" game. I tell him to calm down and say "Stop drawing the devil on the walls. You will bring bad luck." Generally used as a description that someone is foreseeing an impending bad event.

Why? A classical myth held that mentioning the devil would make him appear, which caused a lot of fear, and people avoided mentioning or speaking about him. An old superstition that drawing a symbol on the door will protect the house from the devil led to saying "You don't have to draw on the door, the devil comes into the house by himself." Combined with other superstitions like drawings of the devil will bring him to the house, bringing bad luck and misfortune.

– I want to buy flowers for our friend.
– Why? He must be sick, right?
– Right, how did you guess? You can hear the grass growing.

Das Gras wachsen hören

What? Literally: Hearing the grass grow.
Means: Reading something into it.

How? Of course it is quite clear that growing grass does not make a sound – or does it? – yet still we all have that one friend who might swear that he can definitely hear it. I sure know quite a few fun friends who do. Though, it can also be a recommendation, for example "We have to hear the grass growing, in order to figure out the risks," as in we have to be a bit more diligent. It is used to describe people who are overly obsessive about imaginary problems and are simply "hearing the grass grow."

Why? It dates back all the way to the 15th century as a way to describe wise people who were so aware to the point that they can hear grass growing.
It might also go back to a Scandinavian legend of the elder Edda in poems from the 13th century, in which the Norse guardian of the gods Heimdall is said to have such good ears that he can hear the grass grow on earth.

– I'm a real bottle in this.

Eine Flasche sein

What? Literally: To be a bottle.
Means: To be a loser.

How? "I am such a bottle when it comes to German language." An expression that means someone is very bad at a skill, or completely inadequate. It can also be a swear word "Why did they hire this guy, he is such a bottle?" So be careful when using it, and keep it between you and your close friends when you are hanging out sharing gossip about your annoying neighbor who plays the guitar badly – we will keep it as a secret between us.

Why? An interesting origin story that goes all the way to the past of beautiful Italy. When actors or singers performed badly on the stage, they hung basket bottles on them called "Fiasco", until this term *Fiasco* was used to describe the failed performers themselves. The translation of the word to German is "Korbflasche." This beautiful cultural custom – ironically speaking – eventually migrated to Germany.

+ Note: You might know a similar English term that has the same meaning "Bottlehead".

– Who wants to start first?
– He always wants to play the first violin.

Die erste Geige spielen

What? Literally: To play the first violin.
Means: The desire to be in the spotlight.

How? I am sure you know someone who likes to be the center of attention, at work, or school, or even at a small poetry slam. You signed up for a singing club, and you are all supposed to sing in harmony, except this one person who seems to sing louder and puts extra vowels in the middle of each word to show off his range and skill. "Oh, this person is getting on my nerves, he always wants to play the first violin."

Why? In a string quartet and in every orchestra, the first chairs of the first violins were the most important players who had to set the tone so that other players could orient themselves around them. You can still see this method in all orchestras to this day.

– Hat shop 0815
– Do you like the hat?
– Well, it's pretty much zero eight fifteen.

What? Literally: Something is zero eight fifteen.
Means: It is average, mediocre, nothing special.

How? You might read this in some ads or articles "Our new mountain shoes are not 08/15." An expression that encompasses what would be considered old, outdated, and common. My British hippie friend lives in a van and travels around. "He left the 08/15 job and lifestyle, and now he is living his life freely" – lucky guy.

Why? The term has to do with something completely unexpected, a weapon called 08/15, which was produced around 1908. The term was coined by a German soldier in the Second World War, to say that the weapon was outdated and old. Hence the connection to something being common and out of style.

+ Note: I find it somehow similar to the saying 9 to 5. When people say "I do not want a boring 9 to 5 job."

– Are you visiting him in the hospital?
– He told me through the flower that he'd rather be alone.

Etwas durch die Blume sagen

What? Literally: To say something through the flower.
Means: To say something indirectly.

How? Beating around the bush. You would like to say something that might be a little bit hurtful or share an opinion that could make things awkward, so you say it through the flower. You are hanging out with your friend at your place and it is getting late and you would like to sleep, so you give little hints to your friend by yawning and commenting how late the time is. Your friend is a smart guy and he thinks to himself "Oh, he is telling me to leave through a flower."

Why? A beautiful custom of rejection from a pretty lady. During the medieval dance at the court, the nobleman would go on his knees as a demonstration of his interest in a lady. What would the beautiful lady do if she did not share reciprocal feelings? She would simply hand him a flower as a sign of rejection, to mask the awkwardness of being rejected and the shame. I wish this custom did not die out, it is quite cute.

– He has now bought a townhouse,
– ... an expensive car,
– ... and a garden grill.
– Since he got married.
– He's such a skewerer!

What? Literally: The person carrying a skewer "skewerer" – the tool used for barbecues.
Means: A prudish, close-minded, nitpicking, boring person.

How? Your neighbour is a very boring and close-minded guy. He complains when you make parties, or about you not emptying the trash can on the right day. He likes traditional food, and does not want to try new things "Oh man, my neighbour is such a skewerer." It can also have a similar meaning to being a square. It was used quite often by hippies and alternative cultural groups that rose during the 60s as a derogatory term for the ideal image of a typical boring citizen. It is quite a difficult word to describe, but when you meet this type of person – you will definitely understand.

Why? Back in the days when citizens lived inside fortified cities, they carried spears for security "Spieße". The term became a description for townspeople, who clung to these spears and never dared to cross their fortified city walls. Around the 17th century people started using this term as a mockery referring to these narrow-minded and antiquated people – even up to this day.

SKAPAGO

Online language learning and textbooks.

Herzlichen Glückwunsch!

You have reached the end of the book.
Now you can show off your knowledge of German idioms.
But … there is more.

If you happen to have interest in learning German, then you can check out "Jens und Jakob": the book – which is also available as an online video course – that helped me in my first steps into the language. You will be guided through a story with a structural explanation of the language. It is available in English and Arabic, and hopefully more languages to come.
www.skapago.eu/jensjakob

You might also want to explore other languages with courses from Skapago: **www.skapago.com**.

Tschüss!
Bis nächstes Mal.

Max . Skalla

www.ingramcontent.com/pod-product-compliance
Lightning Source LLC
LaVergne TN
LVHW040104080526
838202LV00045B/3772